W9-CKC-728

REALITY
SANDWICHES

1953 - 60

ALLEN GINSBERG

*'Scribbled secret notebooks, and wild
typewritten pages, for yr own joy'*

CITY LIGHTS BOOKS

© 1963 by Allen Ginsberg

Seventeenth printing, June 1990

ISBN: 0-87286-021-3
LC #63-12219

City Lights Books are available to bookstores through our primary distributor: Subterranean Company. P. O. Box 168, 265 S. 5th St., Monroe, OR 97456. 1-503-847-5274. Toll-free orders 1-800-274-7826. FAX 503-847-6018. Our books are also available through library jobbers and regional distributors. For personal orders and catalogs, please write to City Lights Books, 261 Columbus Avenue, San Francisco CA 94133.

CITY LIGHTS BOOKS are edited by Lawrence Ferlinghetti and Nancy J. Peters and published at the City Lights Bookstore, 261 Columbus Avenue, San Francisco, CA 94133.

Dedicated to
the Pure Imaginary
POET
Gregory Corso

Acknowlegement

Anyone who asked for writings I sent them—the Needle, Provincetown Review, Mattachine Review, Beatitude, Yugen, Evergreen Review, Swank, Partisan Review, White Dove, Chicago Review, i.e. Cambridge Review, New Directions 16, Grecourt Review, Combustion, Folio, Isis, Nomad, Venture, The Beat Scene, Rhinozerous, Hasty Papers, & Between Worlds.

Contents

MY ALBA

Now that I've wasted
five years in Manhattan
life decaying
talent a blank

talking disconnected
patient and mental
sliderule and number
machine on a desk

autographed triplicate
synopsis and taxes
obedient prompt
poorly paid

stayed on the market
youth of my twenties
fainted in offices
wept on typewriters

deceived multitudes
in vast conspiracies
deodorant battleships
serious business industry

every six weeks whoever
drank my blood bank
innocent evil now
part of my system

five years unhappy labor
22 to 27 working
not a dime in the bank
to show for it anyway

dawn breaks it's only the sun
the East smokes O my bedroom
I am damned to Hell what
alarmclock is ringing

NY 1953

SAKYAMUNI COMING OUT FROM THE MOUNTAIN

Liang Kai, Southern Sung

He drags his bare feet
            out of a cave
                        under a tree,
eyebrows
            grown long with weeping
                        and hooknosed woe,
in ragged soft robes
            wearing a fine beard,
                        unhappy hands
clasped to his naked breast—
            humility is beatness
                        humility is beatness—
faltering
            into the bushes by a stream,
                        all things inanimate
but his intelligence—
            stands upright there
                        tho trembling:
Arhat
            who sought Heaven
                        under a mountain of stone,
sat thinking
            till he realized
                        the land of blessedness exists
in the imagination—
            the flash come:
                        empty mirror—

how painful to be born again
                wearing a fine beard,
                                reentering the world
a bitter wreck of a sage:
                earth before him his only path.
                                We can see his soul,
he knows nothing
                like a god:
                                shaken
meek wretch—
                humility is beatness
                                before the absolute World.

NY Public Library 1953

THE GREEN AUTOMOBILE

If I had a Green Automobile
        I'd go find my old companion
        in his house on the Western ocean.
                Ha! Ha! Ha! Ha! Ha!

I'd honk my horn at his manly gate,
        inside his wife and three
        children sprawl naked
                on the living room floor.

He'd come running out
        to my car full of heroic beer
        and jump screaming at the wheel
                for he is the greater driver.

We'd pilgrimage to the highest mount
        of our earlier Rocky Mountain visions
        laughing in each others arms,
                delight surpassing the highest Rockies.

and after old agony, drunk with new years,
        bounding toward the snowy horizon
        blasting the dashboard with original bop
                hot rod on the mountain

we'd batter up the cloudy highway
        where angels of anxiety
        careen through the trees
                and scream out of the engine.

We'd burn all night on the jackpine peak
        seen from Denver in the summer dark,
     forestlike unnatural radiance
           illuminating the mountaintop:

childhood youthtime age & eternity
      would open like sweet trees
      in the nights of another spring
          and dumbfound us with love,

for we can see together
      the beauty of souls
      hidden like diamonds
         in the clock of the world,

like Chinese magicians can
      confound the immortals
      with our intellectuality
         hidden in the mist,

in the Green Automobile
      which I have invented
      imagined and visioned
         on the roads of the world

more real than the engine
      on a track in the desert
      purer than Greyhound and
         swifter than physical jetplane.

Denver! Denver! we'll return
        roaring across the City & County Building lawn
        which catches the pure emerald flame
                streaming in the wake of our auto.

This time we'll buy up the city!
        I cashed a great check in my skull bank
        to found a miraculous college of the body
                up on the bus terminal roof.

But first we'll drive the stations of downtown,
        poolhall flophouse jazzjoint jail
        whorehouse down Folsom
                to the darkest alleys of Larimer

paying respects to Denver's father
        lost on the railroad tracks,
        stupor of wine and silence
                hallowing the slum of his decades,

salute him and his saintly suitcase
        of dark muscatel, drink
        and smash the sweet bottles
                on Diesels in allegiance.

Then we go driving drunk on boulevards
        where armies march and still parade
        staggering under the invisible
                banner of Reality—

hurtling through the street
in the auto of our fate
we share an archangelic cigarette
and tell each others' fortunes:

fames of supernatural illumination,
bleak rainy gaps of time,
great art learned in desolation
and we beat apart after six decades . . .

and on an asphalt crossroad,
deal with each other in princely
gentleness once more, recalling
famous dead talks of other cities.

The windshield's full of tears,
rain wets our naked breasts,
we kneel together in the shade
amid the traffic of night in paradise

and now renew the solitary vow
we made each other take
in Texas, once:
I can't inscribe here . . .
. . . . . .
. . . . . .

How many Saturday nights will be
made drunken by this legend?
How will young Denver come to mourn
her forgotten sexual angel?

How many boys will strike the black piano
   in imitation of the excess of a native saint?
   Or girls fall wanton under his spectre in the high
     schools of melancholy night?

While all the time in Eternity
   in the wan light of this poem's radio
   we'll sit behind forgotten shades
     hearkening the lost jazz of all Saturdays.

Neal, we'll be real heroes now
   in a war between our cocks and time:
   let's be the angels of the world's desire
     and take the world to bed with us before
               we die.

Sleeping alone, or with companion,
   girl or fairy sheep or dream,
   I'll fail of lacklove, you, satiety:
     all men fall, our fathers fell before,

but resurrecting that lost flesh
   is but a moment's work of mind:
   an ageless monument to love
     in the imagination:

memorial built out of our own bodies
   consumed by the invisible poem—
   We'll shudder in Denver and endure
     though blood and wrinkles blind our eyes.

So this Green Automobile:
        I give you in flight
        a present, a present
                from my imagination.

We will go riding
        over the Rockies,
        we'll go on riding
                all night long until dawn,

then back to your railroad, the SP
        your house and your children
        and broken leg destiny
                you'll ride down the plains

in the morning: and back
        to my visions, my office
        and eastern apartment
                I'll return to New York.

NY 1953

HAVANA 1953

I

The night cafe—4AM
     Cuba Libre 20c:
          white tiled squares,
triangular neon lights,
     long wooden bar on one side,
          a great delicatessen booth
on the other facing the street.
     In the center
          among the great city midnight drinkers,
by Aldama Palace
     on Gomez corner,
          white men and women
with standing drums,
     mariachis, voices, guitars—
          drumming on tables,
knives on bottles,
     banging on the floor
          and on each other,
with wooden clacks,
     whistling, howling,
          fat women in strapless silk.

Cop talking to the fat nosed girl
     in a flashy black dress.
          In walks a weird Cezanne
vision of the nowhere hip Cuban:
     tall, thin, check grey suit,
          grey felt shoes,
blaring gambler's hat,

Cab Calloway pimp's mustachio'
—it comes down to a point in the center—
rushing up generations late talking Cuban,
pointing a gold ringed finger
up toward the yellowed ceiling,
other cigarette hand pointing
stiff-armed down at his side,
effeminate:—he sees the cop—
they rush together—they're embracing
like long lost brothers—
fatnose forgotten.

Delicate chords
from the negro guitarino
—singers at El Rancho Grande,
drunken burlesque
screams of agony,
VIVA JALISCO!
I eat a catfish sandwich
with onions and red sauce
20c.

II

A truly romantic spot,
more guitars, Columbus Square
across from Columbus Cathedral
—I'm in the Paris Restaurant
adjacent, best in town,
Cuba Libres 30c—
weatherbeaten tropical antiquity,
as if rock decayed,
unlike the pure

Chinese drummers of black stone
       whose polished harmony can still be heard
              (Procession of Musicians) at the Freer,
this with its blunt cornucopias and horns
       of conquest made of stone—
             a great dumb rotting church.

Night, lights from windows,
       high stone balconies
             on the antique square,
green rooms
       paled by fluorescent houselighting,
            a modern convenience.

I feel rotten.
       I would sit down with my servants and be dumb.
          I spent too much money.

White electricity
       in the gaslamp fixtures of the alley.
          Bullet holes and nails in the stone wall.
The worried headwaiter
       standing amid the potted palms in cans
          in the fifteen foot wooden door looking at me.
Mariachi harmonica artists inside
       getting around to Banjo on My Knee yet.
          They dress in wornout sharpie clothes.

Ancient streetlights down the narrow Calle I face,
       the arch, the square,
          palms, drunkenness, solitude;
voices across the street,

baby wail, girl's squeak,
      waiters nudging each other,
grumble and cackle of young boys' laughter
    in streetcorner waits,
        perro barking off-stage,
baby strangling again,
    banjo and harmonica,
        auto rattle and a cool breeze—

Sudden paranoid notion the waiters are watching me:
    Well they might,
        four gathered in the doorway
and I alone at a table
    on the patio in the dark
        observing the square, drunk.

25c for them
    and I asked for "Jalisco"—
        at the end of the song.

oxcart rolls by
    obtruding its wheels
        o'er the music o' the night.

Christmas 1953

SIESTA IN XBALBA

and

RETURN TO THE STATES

dedicated to Karena Shields

I.

Late sun opening the book,
    blank page like night,
invisible words unscrawled,
    impossible syntax
of apocalypse—
    Uxmal: Noble Ruins
No construction—

    let the mind fall down.

—One could pass valuable months
and years perhaps a lifetime
doing nothing but lying in a hammock
reading prose with the white doves
    copulating underneath
and monkeys barking in the interior
    of the mountain
and I have succumbed to this
    temptation—

'They go mad in the Selva—'
    the madman read
and laughed in his hammock

    eyes watching me:
unease not of the jungle

                    the poor dear,
          can tire one—
                    all that mud
          and all those bugs . . .
                    ugh . . .

          Dreaming back I saw
          an eternal kodachrome
          souvenir of a gathering
          of souls at a party,
          crowded in an oval flash:
          cigarettes, suggestions,
          laughter in drunkenness,
          broken sweet conversation,
          acquaintance in the halls,
          faces posed together,
          stylized gestures
          odd familiar visages
          and singular recognitions
          that registered indifferent
          greeting across time:
          Anson reading Horace
          with a rolling head,
          white-handed Hohnsbean
          camping gravely
          with an absent glance,
          bald Kingsland drinking
          out of a huge glass,
          Dusty in a party dress,
          Durgin in white shoes
          gesturing from a chair,
          Keck in a corner waiting

for subterranean music,
Helen Parker lifting
her hands in surprise:
all posturing in one frame,
superficially gay
or tragic as may be,
illumed with the fatal
character and intelligent
actions of their lives.

And I in a concrete room
                above the abandoned
labyrinth of Palenque
                measuring my fate,
wandering solitary in the wild
                —blinking singleminded
at a bleak idea—
                until exhausted with
its action and contemplation
                my soul might shatter
at one primal moment's
                sensation of the vast
movement of divinity.

As I leaned against a tree
                inside the forest
expiring of self-begotten love,
I looked up at the stars absently,
                as if looking for
something else in the blue night
                through the boughs,
and for a moment saw myself
                leaning against a tree . . .

. . . back there the noise of a great party
in the apartments of New York,
half-created paintings on the walls, fame,
cocksucking and tears,
money and arguments of great affairs,
the culture of my generation . . .

my own crude night imaginings,
my own crude soul notes taken down
in moments of isolation, dreams,
piercings, sequences of nocturnal thought
and primitive illuminations

—uncanny feeling the white cat
sleeping on the table
will open its eyes in a moment
and be looking at me—.

One might sit in this Chiapas
recording the apparitions in the field
visible from a hammock
looking out across the shadow of the pasture
in all the semblance of Eternity

. . . a dwarfed thatch roof
down in the grass in a hollow slope
under the tall crowd of vegetation
waiting at the wild edge:
the long shade of the mountain beyond
in the near distance,
its individual hairline of trees
traced fine and dark along the ridge

    against the transparent sky light,
rifts and holes in the blue air
    and amber brightenings of clouds
disappearing down the other side
     into the South . . .

    palms with lethargic feelers
rattling in presage of rain,
    shifting their fronds
in the direction of the balmy wind,
     monstrous animals
sprayed up out of the ground
    settling and unsettling
as in water . . .
    and later in the night
a moment of premonition
when the plenilunar cloudfilled sky
    is still and small.

So spent a night
    with drug and hammock
at Chichen Itza on the Castle:—

    I can see the moon
moving over the edge of the night forest
    and follow its destination
through the clear dimensions of the sky
    from end to end of the dark
circular horizon.

    High dim stone portals,
entablatures of illegible scripture,

bas-reliefs of unknown perceptions:
                    and now the flicker of my lamp
and smell of kerosene on dust-
                    strewn floor where ant wends
its nightly ritual way toward great faces
                    worn down by rain.
In front of me a deathshead
                    half a thousand years old
—and have seen cocks a thousand
old grown over with moss and batshit
                    stuck out of the wall
in a dripping vaulted house of rock—
                    but deathshead's here
on portal still and thinks its way
                    through centuries the thought
of the same night in which I sit
                    in skully meditation
—sat in many times before by
                    artisan other than me
until his image of ghostly change
                    appeared unalterable—
but now his fine thought's vaguer
                    than my dream of him:
and only the crude skull figurement's
                    gaunt insensible glare is left,
with its broken plumes of sensation
and indecipherable headdresses of intellect
                    scattered in the madness of oblivion
to holes and notes of elemental stone,
blind face of animal transcendency
                    over the holy ruin of the world
dissolving into the sunless wall of a blackened room

on a time-rude pyramid rebuilt
in the bleak flat night of Yucatan
where I come with my own mad mind to study
alien hieroglyphs of Eternity.

A creak in the rooms scared me.

Some sort of bird, vampire or swallow,
flees with little paper wingflap
around the summit in its own air unconcerned
with the great stone tree I perch on.

Continual metallic
whirr of chicharras,
then lesser chirps
of cricket: 5 blasts
of the leg whistle.
The creak of an opening
door in the forest,
some sort of weird birdsong
or reptile croak.

My hat woven of hennequin
on the stone floor
as a leaf on the waters,
as perishable;
my candle wavers continously
and will go out.

Pale Uxmal,
unhistoric, like a dream
Tuluum shimmering on the coast in ruins;

Chichen Itza naked
   constructed on a plain;
Palenque, broken chapels in the green
   basement of a mount;
lone Kabah by the highway;
   Piedras Negras buried again
by dark archaeologists;
   Yaxchilan
resurrected in the wild,
and all the limbo of Xbalba still unknown—

   floors under roofcomb of branch,
foundation to ornament
   tumbled to the flowers,
pyramids and stairways
   raced with vine,
limestone corbels,
   down in the river of trees,
pillars and corridors
   sunken under the flood of years:

Time's slow wall overtopping
   all that firmament of mind,
as if a shining waterfall of leaves and rain
were built down solid from the endless sky
   through which no thought can pass.

A great red fat rooster
mounted on a tree stump
in the green afternoon,
the ego of the very fields,
screams in the holy sunlight!

—I can't think with that
supersonic cock intensity
crucifying my skull
in its imaginary sleep.

        —was looking back
with eyes shut to
        where they crawled
like ants on brown old temples
        building their minute ruins
and disappearing into the wild
        leaving many mysteries
of deathly volition
        to be divined.

I alone know the great crystal door
        to the House of Night,
a legend of centuries
        —I and a few Indians.

And had I mules and money I could find
        the Cave of Amber
and the Cave of Gold
        rumored of the cliffs of Tumbala.

I found the face of one
        of the Nine Guardians of the Night
hidden in a mahogany hut
        in the Area of Lost Souls
—first relic of kind for that place.

And I found as well a green leaf
                shaped like a human heart;
but to whom shall I send this
                anachronistic valentine?

Yet these ruins so much
                woke me to nostalgia
for the classic stations
                of the earth,
the ancient continent
                I have not seen
and the few years
                of memory left
before the ultimate night
                of war.

As if these ruins were not enough,
                as if man could go
no further before heaven
                till he exhausted
the physical round
                of his own mortality
in the obscure cities
                hidden in the ageing world

    . . . the few actual
                ecstatic conscious souls
certain to be found,
                familiars . . .

returning after years
        to my own scene
transfigured:
        to hurry change
to hurry the years
        bring me to my fate.

So I dream nightly of an embarcation,
        captains, captains,
iron passageways, cabin lights,
        Brooklyn across the waters,
the great dull boat, visitors, farewells,
        the blurred vast sea—
one trip a lifetime's loss or gain:

as Europe is my own imagination
        —many shall see her,
        many shall not—
though it's only the old familiar world
and not some abstract mystical dream.

And in a moment of previsioning sleep
        I see that continent in rain,
black streets, old night, a
        fading monument . . .

And a long journey unaccomplished
        yet, on antique seas
rolling in gray barren dunes under
        the world's waste of light
toward ports of childish geography

        the rusty ship will
harbor in . . .

What nights might I not see
        penniless among the Arab
mysteries of dirty towns around
        the casbahs of the docks?
Clay paths, mud walls,
        the smell of green cigarettes,
creosote and rank salt water—
        dark structures overhead,
shapes of machinery and facade
        of hull: and a bar lamp
burning in the wooden shack
        across from the dim
mountain of sulphur on the pier.

        Toward what city
will I travel? What wild houses
        do I go to occupy?
What vagrant rooms and streets
        and lights in the long night
urge my expectation? What genius
        of sensation in ancient
halls? what jazz beyond jazz
        in future blue saloons?
what love in the cafes of God?

I thought, five years ago
        sitting in my apartment,
my eyes were opened for an hour
        seeing in dreadful ecstasy

the motionless buildings
            of New York rotting
under the tides of Heaven.

There is a god
dying in America
already created
in the imagination of men
made palpable
for adoration:
there is an inner
anterior image
of divinity
beckoning me out
to pilgrimage.

O future, unimaginable God.

> *Finca Tacalapan de San*
> *Leandro, Palenque,*
> *Chiapas, Mexico 1954—*
> *San Francisco 1955*

II.

Jump in time
            to the immediate future,
another poem:

            return to the old land
penniless and with
            a disconnected manuscript,

the recollection of a few
        sensations, beginning:

logboat down Rio Michol
        under plantain
and drifting trees
        to the railroad,

        darkness on the sea
looking toward the stations
        of the classic world—

another image descending
        in white mist
down the lunar highway
        at dawn, above
Lake Catemaco on the bus
        —it woke me up—
the far away likeness
        of a heavenly file
of female saints
        stepping upward
on miniature arches
        of a gold stairway
into the starry sky,
        the thousands of little
saintesses in blue hoods
        looking out at me
and beckoning:
        SALVATION!

It's true,
simple as in the image.

Then the mummies
in their Pantheon
at Guanajuato—
a city of Cortesian
mines in the first
crevasse of the Sierras
where I rested—

for I longed to see their
faces before I left:
these weren't mythical rock
images, tho stone
—limestone effigies out
of the grave, remains
of the fatal character—

newly resurrected,
grasping their bodies
with stiff arms, in soiled
funeral clothes;
twisted, knock-kneed
like burning
screaming lawyers—
what hallucinations
of the nerves?—
indecipherable-sexed;
one death-man had
raised up his arms
to cover his eyes,

significant timeless
            reflex in sepulchre:

apparitions of immortality
            consumed inward,
waiting openmouthed
            in the fireless darkness.
Nearby, stacked symmetrically,
            a skullbone wall ending
the whitewashed corridor
            under the graveyard
—foetid smell reminiscent
            of sperm and drunkenness—
the skulls empty and fragile,
            numerous as shells,
—so much life passed through
            this town . . .

The problem is isolation
            —there in the grave
or here in oblivion of light.

            Of eternity we have
a numbered score of years
            and fewer tender moments
—one moment of tenderness
            and a year of intelligence
and nerves: one moment of pure
            bodily tenderness—
I could dismiss Allen with grim
            pleasure.

Reminder: I knelt in my room
        on the patio at San Miguel
at the keyhole: 2 A.M.
        The old woman lit a candle.
Two young men and their girls
        waited before the portal,
news from the street. She
        changed the linen, smiling.

What joy! The nakedness!
        They dance! They talk
and simper before the door,
        they lean on a leg,
hand on a hip, and posture,
        nudity in their hearts,
they clap a hand to head
        and whirl and enter,
pushing each other,
        happily, happily,
to a moment of love . . .

What solitude I've
        finally inherited.

        Afterward fifteen hours
on rubbled single lane,
        broken bus rocking along
the maws and continental crags
        of mountain afternoon,
the distant valleys fading,
        regnant peaks beyond

to days on the Pacific
>where I bathed—

then riding, fitful,
>gazing, sleeping
through the desert
>beside a wetback
sad-faced old-man-
>youth, exhausted
to Mexicali

>to stand
near one night's dark shack
>on the garbage cliffs
of bordertown overhanging
>the tin house poor
man's village below,
>a last night's
timewracked brooding
>and farewell,
the end of a trip.

—Returning
>armed with New Testament,
critic of horse and mule,
>tanned and bearded
satisfying Whitman, concerned
>with a few Traditions,
metrical, mystical, manly
. . . and certain characteristic flaws

>—enough!

The nation over the border
grinds its arms and dreams
        of war: I see
the fiery blue clash
        of metal wheels
clanking in the industries
        of night, and
detonation of infernal bombs

        . . . and the silent downtown
of the States
        in watery dusk submersion.

Guanajuato—Los Angeles, 1954

[NOTE: *Uxmal and other proper names mentioned in the first part of the
poem are those of ruined cities. Xbalba, translatable as morning Star in
Region Obscure, or Hope, and pronounced Chivalvá, is the area in Chiapas
between the Tobasco border and the Usumascintla River at the edge of the
Peten Rain Forest; the boundary of lower Mexico and Guatemala today is
thereabouts. The locale was considered a Purgatory or Limbo, the legend is
vague, in the (Old) Mayan Empire. To the large tree at the crest of what is
now called Mount Don Juan, at the foot of which this poem was written,
ancient craftsmen came to complete work left unfinished at their death. .*]

ON BURROUGHS' WORK

The method must be purest meat
        and no symbolic dressing,
actual visions & actual prisons
        as seen then and now.

Prisons and visions presented
        with rare descriptions
corresponding exactly to those
        of Alcatraz and Rose.

A naked lunch is natural to us,
        we eat reality sandwiches.
But allegories are so much lettuce.
        Don't hide the madness.

San Jose 1954

LOVE POEM ON THEME BY WHITMAN

I'll go into the bedroom silently and lie down between the
    bridegroom and the bride,
those bodies fallen from heaven stretched out waiting naked and
    restless,
arms resting over their eyes in the darkness,
bury my face in their shoulders and breasts, breathing their skin,
and stroke and kiss neck and mouth and make back be open
    and known,
legs raised up crook'd to receive, cock in the darkness driven
    tormented and attacking
roused up from hole to itching head,
bodies locked shuddering naked, hot hips and buttocks screwed
    into each other
and eyes, eyes glinting and charming, widening into looks and
    abandon,
and moans of movement, voices, hands in air, hands between
    thighs,
hands in moisture on softened hips, throbbing contraction of
    bellies
till the white come flow in the swirling sheets,
and the bride cry for forgiveness, and the groom be covered with
    tears of passion and compassion,
and I rise up from the bed replenished with last intimate gestures
    and kisses of farewell—
all before the mind wakes, behind shades and closed doors in a
    darkened house
where the inhabitants roam unsatisfied in the night,
nude ghosts seeking each other out in the silence.

OVER KANSAS

Starting with eyeball kicks
on storefronts from bus window
on way to Oakland airport:
I am no ego

        these are themselves
stained grey wood and gilded
nigger glass and barberpole

        thass all.
But then, Kiss Me Again
in the dim brick lounge,
muted modern music.
Where shall I fly
not to be sad, my dear?
The other businessmen
bend heavily over armchairs
introducing women to cocktails
in fluorescent shadow—
gaiety of tables,

        gaiety of fat necks,
gaiety of departures,
gaiety of national business,
hands waving away jokes.

        I'm getting maudlin
on the soft rug watching,
mixed rye before me
on the little black table
whereon lieth my briefcase
containing market research
notes and blank paper—
that airplane ride to come

—or a barefaced pilgrimage
acrost imaginary plains
I never made afoot
into Kansas hallucination
and supernatural deliverance.

Later: Hawthorne mystic
waiting on the bench
composing his sermon also
with white bony fingers
bitten, with hometown gold
ring, in a blue serge suit
and barely visible blond
mustache on mental face,
blank-eyed: pitiful thin body
—what body may he love?—
My God! the soft beauty in
comparison—that football boy
in sunny yellow lovesuit
puzzling out his Xmas trip
death insurance by machine.
A virginal feeling again,
I'd be willing to die aloft now.

Can't see outside in the dark,
real dreary strangers about
and I'm unhappy flying away.
All this facility of travel
too superficial for the heart
I have for solitude.
                              Nakedness

must come again—not sex,
but some naked isolation.

And down there's Hollywood,
the starry world below
—expressing nakedness—
that craving, that glory
that applause—leisure, mind,
appetite for dreams, bodies,
travels: appetite for the real,
created by the mind
and kissed in coitus—
that craving, that melting!
Not even the human
imagination satisfies
the endless emptiness of the soul.

The West Coast behind me
for five days while I return
to ancient New York—
ah drunkenness!
I'll see your eyes again.
Hopeless comedown!
Travelling thru the dark void
over Kansas yet moving nowhere
in the dark void of the soul.

Angel woke me to see
—past my own reflection,
bald businessman with hornrims
sleepy in round window view—
spectral skeleton of electricity

illuminated nervous system
floating on the void out
of central brainplant powerhouse
running into heaven's starlight
overhead. 'Twas over Hutchinson,
Engine passed over lights,
                    view gone.

Gorgeous George on my plane.

And Chicago, the first time,
smoking winter city
—shivering in my tweed jacket
walking by the airport
around the block on Cicero
under the fogged flat
supersky of heaven—
another project for the heart,
six months for here someday
to make Chicago natural,
pick up a few strange images.

Far off red signs
on the orphan highway
glimmer at the trucks of home.
Who rides that lone road now?
What heart? Who smokes and loves
in Kansas auto now?
Who's talking magic
under the night? Who walks
downtown and drinks black beer
in his eternity? Whose eyes

collect the streets and mountain tops
for storage in his memory?
What sage in the darkness?

Someone who should collect
my insurance!
             Better I make
a thornful pilgrimage on theory
feet to suffer the total
isolation of the bum,
than this hipster
business family journey
—crossing U.S. at night—
in a sudden glimpse
me being no one in the air
nothing but clouds in the moonlight
with humans fucking
underneath . . .

SF-NY December 1954

MALEST CORNIFICI TUO CATULLO

I'm happy, Kerouac, your madman Allen's
finally made it: discovered a new young cat,
and my imagination of an eternal boy
walks on the streets of San Francisco,
handsome, and meets me in cafeterias
and loves me. Ah don't think I'm sickening.
You're angry at me. For all of my lovers?
It's hard to eat shit, without having visions;
when they have eyes for me it's like Heaven.

SF 1955

DREAM RECORD : JUNE 8, 1955

A drunken night in my house with a
boy, San Francisco: I lay asleep:
darkness:

       I went back to Mexico City
and saw Joan Burroughs leaning
forward in a garden-chair, arms
on her knees. She studied me with
clear eyes and downcast smile, her
face restored to a fine beauty
tequila and salt had made strange
before the bullet in her brow.

We talked of the life since then.
Well, what's Burroughs doing now?
Bill on earth, he's in North Africa.
Oh, and Kerouac? Jack still jumps
with the same beat genius as before,
notebooks filled with Buddha.
I hope he makes it, she laughed.
Is Huncke still in the can? No,
last time I saw him on Times Square.
And how is Kenney? Married, drunk
and golden in the East. You? New
loves in the West—

       Then I knew
she was a dream : and questioned her
—Joan, what kind of knowledge have
the dead? can you still love
your mortal acquaintances?
What do you remember of us?

                               She
faded in front of me—The next instant
I saw her rain-stained tombstone
rear an illegible epitaph
under the gnarled branch of a small
tree in the wild grass
of an unvisited garden in Mexico.

*   *   *

Blessed be the Muses
    for their descent,
dancing round my desk,
crowning my balding head
    with Laurel.

*   *   *

FRAGMENT 1956

Now to the come of the poem, let me be worthy
& sing holily the natural pathos of the human soul,
naked original skin beneath our dreams
& robes of thought, the perfect self identity
radiant with lusts and intellectual faces
Who carries the lines, the painful browed
contortions of the upper eyes, the whole body
breathing and sentient among flowers and buildings
open-eyed, self knowing, trembling with love—
Soul that I have, that Jack has, Huncke has
Bill has, Joan had, and has in me memory yet,
bum has in rags, madman underneath black clothes.
Soul identical each to each, as standing on
the streetcorner ten years ago I looked at Jack
and told him we were the same person—look
in my eyes and speak to yourself, that makes me
everybody's lover, Hal mine against his will,
I had his soul in my own body already, while
he frowned—by the streetlamp 8th Avenue & 27th
Street 1947—I had just come back from Africa
with a gleam of the illumination actually
to come to me in time as come to all—Jack
the worst murderer, Allen the most cowardly
with a streak of yellow love running through
my poems, a fag in the city, Joe Army screaming
in anguish in Dannemora 1945 jailhouse,
breaking his own white knuckle against the bars
his dumb sad cellmate beaten by the guards
an iron floor below, Gregory weeping in Tombs,
Joan lidded under eyes of benzedrine

harkening to the paranoia in the wall,
Huncke from Chicago dreaming in Arcades
of hellish Pokerino blue skinned Times Square light,
Bill King yelling pale faced in the subway window
final minute gape-death struggling to return,
Morphy himself, arch suicide, expiring in blood
on the Passaic, tragic & bewildered in
last tears, attaining death that moment
human, intellectual, bearded, who else
was he then but himself?

Berkeley, 1956

A STRANGE NEW COTTAGE IN BERKELEY

All afternoon cutting bramble blackberries off a tottering
brown fence
under a low branch with its rotten old apricots miscellaneous
under the leaves,
fixing the drip in the intricate gut machinery of a new toilet;
found a good coffeepot in the vines by the porch, rolled a
big tire out of the scarlet bushes, hid my marijuana;
wet the flowers, playing the sunlit water each to each,
returning for godly extra drops for the stringbeans and daisies;
three times walked round the grass and sighed absently:
my reward, when the garden fed me its plums from the
form of a small tree in the corner,
an angel thoughtful of my stomach, and my dry and love-
lorn tongue.

1956

SATHER GATE ILLUMINATION

Why do I deny manna to another?
Because I deny it to myself.
Why have I denied myself?
What other has rejected me?
Now I believe you are lovely, my soul, soul of Allen, Allen—
and you so beloved, so sweetened, so recalled to your true loveli-
ness,
your original nude breathing Allen
will you ever deny another again?

Dear Walter, thanks for the message
I forbid you not to touch me, man to man, True American.

The bombers jet through the sky in unison of twelve,
the pilots are sweating and nervous at the controls in the hot
cabins.
Over what souls will they loose their loveless bombs?

The Campanile pokes its white granite (?) innocent head into
the clouds for me to look at.

A cripple lady explains French grammar with a loud sweet voice:
Regarder is to look—
the whole French language looks on the tree on the campus.

The girls' haunted voices make quiet dates for 2 o'clock
—yet one of them waves farewell and smiles at last—her red
skirt swinging shows how she loves herself.

Another encased in flashy Scotch clothes clomps up the

concrete in a hurry—into the door—poor dear!—who will
receive you in love's offices?

How many beautiful boys have I seen on this spot?
The trees seem on the verge of moving—ah! they do move in
        the breeze.
Roar again of airplanes in the sky—everyone looks up.

And do you know that all these rubbings of the eyes & painful
        gestures to the brow
of suited scholars entering Dwinelle (Hall) are Holy Signs?—
        anxiety and fear?

How many years have I got to float on this sweetened scene of
        trees & humans clomping above ground—
O I must be mad to sit here lonely in the void & glee & build
        up thoughts of love!
But what do I have to doubt but my own shiney eyes, what to
        lose but life which is a vision today this afternoon.

        My stomach is light, I relax, new sentences spring
forth out of the scene to describe spontaneous forms of Time
—trees, sleeping dogs, airplanes wandering thru the air, negroes
with their lunch books of anxiety, apples and sandwiches, lunch-
time, icecream, Timeless—

And even the ugliest will seek beauty—'What are you doing
        Friday night?'
asks the sailor in white school training cap & gilt buttons & blue
        coat,
and the little ape in a green jacket and baggy pants and over-
        loaded schoolbook satchel says 'Quartets.'

Every Friday nite, beautiful quartets to celebrate and please my
soul with all its hair—Music!
and then strides off, snapping pieces chocolate off a bar wrapped
in Hershey brown paper and tinfoil,
eating chocolate rose.

& how can those other boys be them happy selves in their brown
army study uniforms?

Now cripple girl swings down walk with loping fuck gestures of
her hips askew—
let her roll her eyes in abandon & camp angelic through the
campus bouncing her body about in joy—
someone will dig that pelvic energy for sure.

Those white stripes down your chocolate cupcake, Lady (held
in front of your nose finishing sentence preparatory
to chomp),
they were painted there to delight you by some spanish industrial
artistic hand in bakery factory faraway,
expert hand in simple-minded messages of white stripes on
millions of message cupcakes.

I have a message for you all—I will denote one particularity
of each!

And there goes Professor Hart striding enlightened by
the years through the doorway and arcade he built (in his mind)
and knows—he too saw the ruins of Yucatan once—

followed by a lonely janitor in dovegrey italian fruitpeddlar
Chico Marx hat pushing his rollypoly belly thru the
trees.

N sees all girls
as visions of
their inner cunts,
yes, it's true!
and all men walking
along thinking
of their spirit cocks.

So look at that poor dread boy
with two-day black hair
all over his dirty face,
how he must hate his cock
        —Chinamen stop shuddering

        and now to bring this to an end with a rise and an
ellipse—

        The boys are now all talking to the girls 'If I was a
girl I'd love all boys' & girls giggling the opposite, all pretty
everywhichway
and even I have my secret beds and lovers under another moon-
        light, be you sure

& any minute I expect to see a baby carriage pushed on to the
        scene
and everyone turn in attention like the airplanes and laughter,
        like a Greek Campus
and the big brown shaggy silent dog lazing openeyed in the shade
lift up his head & sniff & lower his head on his golden paws
        & let his belly rumble away unconcerned.

> . . . The lion's ruddy eyes
Shall flow with tears of gold.

Now the silence is broken, students pour onto the square, the
        doors are crowded, the dog gets up and walks away,
the cripple swings out of Dwinelle, a nun even, I wonder about
        her, an old lady distinguished by a cane,
we all look up, silence moves, huge changes upon the ground,
        and in the air thoughts fly all over filling space.

My grief at Peter's not loving me was grief at not loving myself.
Huge Karmas of broken minds in beautiful bodies unable to
        receive love because not knowing the self as lovely—
Fathers and Teachers!

        Seeing in people the visible evidence of inner self
thought by their treatment of me: who loves himself loves me
who love myself.

Berkeley, September 1956

SCRIBBLE

Rexroth's face reflecting human
      tired bliss
White haired, wing browed
      gas mustache,
         flowers jet out of
            his sad head,
listening to Edith Piaf street song
      as she walks the universe
         with all life gone
         and cities disappeared
            only the God of Love
              left smiling.

Berkeley, March 1956

AFTERNOON SEATTLE

Busride along waterfront down Yessler under street bridge
to the old red Wobbly Hall—
One Big Union, posters of the Great Mandala of Labor,
bleareyed dusty cardplayers dreaming behind the counter . . .
'but these young fellers can't see ahead and we nothing to
offer'—
After Snyder his little red beard and bristling Buddha mind
I weeping crossed Skid Road to 10c. beer.
Labyrinth wood stairways and Greek movies under Farmers
Market second hand city, Indian smoked salmon old overcoats
and dry red shoes,
Green Parrot Theater, *Maytime,* and down to the harborside
the ships, walked on Alaska silent together—ferryboat coming
faraway in mist from Bremerton Island dreamlike small on the
waters of Holland to me
—and entered my head the seagull, a shriek, sentinels
standing over rusty harbor iron dockwork, rocks dripping under
rotten wharves slime on the walls—
the seagull's small cry—inhuman not of the city, lone
sentinels of God, animal birds among us indifferent, their bleak
lone cries representing our souls.
A rowboat docked and chained floating in the tide by a
wharf. Basho's frog. Someone left it there, it drifts.
Sailor's curio shop hung with shells and skulls a whalebone
mask, Indian seas. The cities rot from oldest parts. Little red
mummy from Idaho Frank H. Little your big hat high cheek-
bones crosseyes and song.
The cities rot from the center, the suburbs fall apart a slow
apocalypse of rot the special trolleys fade
the cities rot the fire escapes hang and rust the brick turns

black dust falls uncollected garbage heaps the wall

the birds invade with their cries the skid row alley creeps downtown the ancient jailhouse groans bums snore under the pavement a dark Turkish bath the cornice gapes at midnight

Seattle!—department stores full of fur coats and camping equipment, mad noontime businessmen in gabardine coats talking on streetcorners to keep up the structure, I float past, birds cry,

Salvation Army offers soup on rotting block, six thousand beggars groan at a meal of hopeful beans.

February 2, 1956

PSALM III

To God : to illuminate all men. Beginning with Skid Road.

Let Occidental and Washington be transformed into a higher place, the plaza of eternity.

Illuminate the welders in shipyards with the brilliance of their torches.

Let the crane operator lift up his arm for joy.

Let elevators creak and speak, ascending and descending in awe.

Let the mercy of the flower's direction beckon in the eye.

Let the straight flower bespeak its purpose in straightness— to seek the light.

Let the crooked flower bespeak its purpose in crookedness— to seek the light.

Let the crookedness and straightness bespeak the light.

Let Puget Sound be a blast of light.

I feed on your Name like a cockroach on a crumb—this cockroach is holy.

Seattle, June 1956

TEARS

I'm crying all the time now.
I cried all over the street when I left the Seattle Wobbly Hall.
I cried listening to Bach.
I cried looking at the happy flowers in my backyard, I cried at
      the sadness of the middle-aged trees.

Happiness exists I feel it.
I cried for my soul, I cried for the world's soul.
The world has a beautiful soul.
God appearing to be seen and cried over. Overflowing heart of
      Paterson.

Seattle, February 2, 1956

READY TO ROLL

To Mexico! To Mexico! Down the dovegrey highway, past
    Atomic City police, past the firey border to dream
    cantinas!
Standing on the sunny metropolitan plateau, stranger prince
    on the street, dollars in my pocket, alone, free—
    genitals and thighs and buttocks under skin and
    leather.
Music! Taxis! Marijuana in the slums! Ancient sexy parks!
    Continental boulevards in America! Modern downtown
    for a dollar! Dungarees in Les Ambassadeurs! And
    here's a hard brown cock for a quarter!
Drunkenness! and the long night walks down brown streets,
    eyes, windows, buses, interior charnels behind the
    Cathedral, lost squares and hungry tacos, a calf's head
    cooked and picked apart for meat,
and the blackened inner roofs and tents of the Thieves'
    Market, street crisscrossed on street, a naked hipster
    labyrinth, stealing, pausing, loitering, noticing drums,
    purchasing nothing
but a broken aluminum coffee pot with a doll's arm sticking
    up out of the mouth.
Haha! what do I want? Change of solitude, spectre of
    drunkenness in paranoiac taxicabs, fear and gaiety of
    unknown lovers
coming around the empty streetcorner dark-eyed and watching
    me make it there alone under the new hip moon.

San Francisco, October 1956

WROTE THIS LAST NIGHT

Listen to the tale of the sensitive car
who was coughed up out of earth in Pittsburgh.

She screamed like a Swedish Prime Minister
on her first flight down the red neon highway,

she couldn't stand the sirens and blind lights
of the male cars Fords Oldsmobiles Studebakers

—her assembly line foreman had prophesied wild wreck
on Sunset Boulevard headlights & eyeballs broken fenders &
      bones.

She rode all over Mexico avoiding Los Angeles
praying to be an old junkie in a bordertown graveyard

with rattley doors and yellow broken windowpanes
bent license plate weak brakes & unsalable motor

worn out by the slow buttocks of teen-age nightmare
panting under the impoverished jissum of the August moon,

Anything but that final joyride with the mad producer
and his bombshell intellectual star on the last night up from
      Mexicali.

Paris, December 1957

SQUEAL

He rises he stretches he liquefies he is hammered again
He's divided in shares he litters the floor of the Bourse
He's cut by adamantine snips and sent by railway car
Accumulated on the margin by bony Goldfinger has various
Visions of being an automobile consolidates
The fortune of spectral lawyers heirs weep over him
He melts he undergoes remarkable metamorphoses peculiar
Hallucinations he coughs up debentures beaten
By immense hammers in a vast loft pours in fire spurts
Upward in molten forges he levels he dreams and he cools
And the present adjusted steel squints.

A hunchback tuberculosis salesman drives him cackling to St
    Louis
In the rain Hack no will of his own Creep next resale Crank
San Pedro tomorrow St Joe Squeak will it never end Hohokus—

Crashes into a dirty locomotive the bastard never
Mind stock averages decline slightly here's the mechanic
Blam the junkyard Help the smelter later a merger pressure
    accumulates
He's had it now Eek he's an airplane Whine he wants to go home
Suddenly he dives on the market like a bomb.

Paris, December 1957

AMERICAN CHANGE

The first I looked on, after a long time far from home in mid Atlantic on a summer day

Dolphins breaking the glassy water under the blue sky,

a gleam of silver in my cabin, fished up out of my jangling new pocket of coins and green dollars

—held in my palm, the head of the feathered Indian, old Buck-Rogers eagle eyed face, a gash of hunger in the cheek

gritted jaw of the vanished man begone like a Hebrew with hairlock combed down the side—O Rabbi Indian

what visionary gleam 100 years ago on Buffalo prairie under the molten cloud shot sky, 'the same clear light 10000 miles in all directions'

but now with all the violin music of Vienna, gone into the great slot machine of Kansas City, Reno—

The coin seemed so small after vast European coppers thick francs leaden pesetas, lira endless and heavy,

a miniature primeval memorialized in 5c. nickle candystore nostalgia of the redskin, dead on silver coin,

with shaggy buffalo on reverse, hump-backed little tail incurved, head butting against the rondure of Eternity,

cock forelock below, bearded shoulder muscle folded below muscle, head of prophet, bowed,

vanishing beast of Time, hoar body rubbed clean of wrinkles and shining like polished stone, bright metal in my forefinger, ridiculous buffalo—Go to New York.

Dime next I found, Minerva, sexless cold & chill, ascending goddess of money—and was it the wife of Wallace Stevens, truly?

and now from the locks flowing the miniature wings of speedy thought,

executive dyke, Minerva, goddess of Madison Avenue, forgotten useless dime that can't buy hot dog, dead dime—

Then we've George Washington, less primitive, the snub-nosed quarter, smug eyes and mouth, some idiot's design of the sexless Father,

naked down to his neck, a ribbon in his wig, high fore-head, Roman line down the nose, fat cheeked, still showing his falsetooth ideas—O Eisenhower & Washington—O Fathers— No movie star dark beauty—O thou Bignoses—

Quarter, remembered quarter, 40c. in all—What'll you buy me when I land—one icecream soda?—

poor pile of coins, original reminders of the sadness, forgotten money of America—

nostalgia of the first touch of those coins, American change,

the memory in my aging hand, the same old silver reflec-tive there,

the thin dime hidden between my thumb and forefinger

All the struggles for those coins, the sadness of their re-appearance

my reappearance on those fabled shores

and the failure of that Dream, that Vision of Money reduced to this haunting recollection

of the gas lot in Paterson where I found half a dollar gleaming in the grass—

I have a $5 bill in my pocket—it's Lincoln's sour black head moled wrinkled, forelocked too, big eared, flags of announce-ment flying over the bill, stamps in green and spiderweb black, long numbers in racetrack green, immense promise, a girl, a hotel, a busride to Albany, a night of brilliant drunk in some faraway corner of Manhattan

a stick of several teas, or paper or cap of Heroin, or a $5 strange present to the blind.

Money money, reminder, I might as well write poems to you—dear American money—O statue of Liberty I ride enfolded in money in my mind to you—and last

Ahhh! Washington again, on the Dollar, same poetic black print, dark words, The United States of America, innumerable numbers

R956422481 One Dollar This Certificate is Legal Tender (tender!) for all debts public and private

My God My God why have you forsaken me

Ivy Baker Priest Series 1935 F

and over, the Eagle, wild wings outspread, halo of the Stars encircled by puffs of smoke & flame—

a circle the Masonic Pyramid the sacred Swedenborgian Dollar America, bricked up to the top, & floating surreal above

the triangle of holy outstaring Eye sectioned out of the aire, shining

light emitted from the eyebrowless triangle—and a desert of cactus, scattered all around, clouds afar,

this being the Great Seal of our Passion, Annuit Coeptis, Novus Ordo Seclorum,

the whole surrounded by green spiderwebs designed by T-Men to prevent foul counterfeit—

ONE

S.S. United States, July 1958

'BACK ON TIMES SQUARE,
DREAMING OF TIMES SQUARE'

Let some sad trumpeter stand
        on the empty streets at dawn
and blow a silver chorus to the
        buildings of Times Square,
memorial of ten years, at 5 AM, with
        the thin white moon just
            visible
     above the green & grooking McGraw
        Hill offices

a cop walks by, but he's invisible
        with his music

The Globe Hotel, Garver lay in
      grey beds there and hunched his
      back and cleaned his needles—
where I lay many nights on the nod
      from his leftover bloody cottons
      and dreamed of Blake's voice talking—
           I was lonely,
      Garver's dead in Mexico two years,
    hotel's vanished into a parking lot
And I'm back here—sitting on the streets
again—

      The movies took our language, the
         great red signs
       A DOUBLE BILL OF GASSERS
        Teen Age Nightmare
        Hooligans of the Moon

But we were never nightmare
　　　hooligans but seekers of
　　　　　the blond nose for Truth

Some old men are still alive, but
　　　　　the old Junkies are gone—

We are a legend, invisible but
　　　　　legendary, as prophesied

New York, July 1958

MY SAD SELF

To Frank O'Hara

Sometimes when my eyes are red
I go up on top of the RCA Building
  and gaze at my world, Manhattan—
     my buildings, streets I've done feats in,
      lofts, beds, coldwater flats
—on Fifth Ave below which I also bear in mind,
  its ant cars, little yellow taxis, men
    walking the size of specks of wool—
Panorama of the bridges, sunrise over Brooklyn machine,
  sun go down over New Jersey where I was born
    & Paterson where I played with ants—
my later loves on 15th Street,
  my greater loves of Lower East Side,
    my once fabulous amours in the Bronx
      faraway—
paths crossing in these hidden streets,
  my history summed up, my absences
    and ecstasies in Harlem—
  —sun shining down on all I own
    in one eyeblink to the horizon
      in my last eternity—
        matter is water.

Sad,
  I take the elevator and go
    down, pondering,
and walk on the pavements staring into all man's
        plateglass, faces,
    questioning after who loves,

and stop, bemused
    in front of an automobile shopwindow
standing lost in calm thought,
      traffic moving up & down 5th Avenue blocks
          behind me
      waiting for a moment when . . .

Time to go home & cook supper & listen to
            the romantic war news on the radio

                . . . all movement stops
& I walk in the timeless sadness of existence,
    tenderness flowing thru the buildings,
      my fingertips touching reality's face,
    my own face streaked with tears in the mirror
    of some window—at dusk—
          where I have no desire—
for bonbons—or to own the dresses or Japanese
    lampshades of intellection—

Confused by the spectacle around me,
    Man struggling up the street
      with packages, newspapers,
          ties, beautiful suits
      toward his desire
    Man, woman, streaming over the pavements
      red lights clocking hurried watches &
      movements at the curb—

And all these streets leading
    so crosswise, honking, lengthily,
      by avenues

        stalked by high buildings or crusted into slums
              thru such halting traffic
                       screaming cars and engines
so painfully to this
      countryside, this graveyard
            this stillness
                      on deathbed or mountain
      once seen
              never regained or desired
                    in the mind to come
where all Manhattan that I've seen must disappear.

New York, October 1958

```
FFFFF  U           U   NN     N
F      U           U   N N    N
FFFFF  U           U   N  N   N
F        U     U   N    N N  N  NY      DEATH
F          U  U    N        NN
F           UU     N         N
```

The music of the spheres—that ends in Silence
The Void is a grand piano
                        a million melodies
                    one after another
            silence in between
                        rather an interruption
                        of the silence

                        Tho the music's beautiful
Bong Bong Bon————
                    gnob
                        gnob
                            gno————

    Bong Bong Bong
    o   n
    n   o
    g   b
    b   g
    o   n
    n   o
    obgnobgnobgnob
                        THE circle of forms
                        Shrinks
                            and disappears
                        back into the piano.

New York, September 25, 1958

BATTLESHIP NEWSREEL

I was high on tea in my foc'sle near the forepeak hatch listening
     to the stars

envisioning the kamakazis flapping and turning in the soiled
     clouds

ackack burst into fire a vast hole ripped out of the bow like a
     burning lily

we dumped our oilcans of nitroglycerine among the waving
     octopi

dull thud and boom of thunder undersea the cough of the
     tubercular machinegunner

flames in the hold among the cans of ether the roar of battleships
     far away

rolling in the sea like whales surrounded by dying ants the
     screams the captain mad

Suddenly a golden light came over the ocean and grew large the
     radiance entered the sky

a deathly chill and heaviness entered my body I could scarce lift
     my eye

and the ship grew sheathed in light like an overexposed photo-
     graph fading in the brain.

New York, 1959

I BEG YOU TO COME BACK & BE CHEERFUL

Tonite I got hi in the window of my apartment
                    chair at 3 : A.M.
gazing at Blue incandescent torches
                    bright-lit street below
clotted shadows looming on a new laid pave
—as last week Medieval rabbiz
                    plodded thru the brown raw
                    dirt turned over—sticks
                              & cans
and tired ladies sitting on spanish
                    garbage pails—in the deadly heat
                              —one month ago
                    the fire hydrants were awash—
the sun at 3 P.M. today in a haze—
now all dark outside, a cat crosses
                    the street silently—I meow
and she looks up, and passes a
                    pile of rubble on the way
to a golden shining garbage pail
                    (phosphor in the night
                              & alley stink)
                    (or door-can mash)
—Thinking America is a chaos
Police clog the streets with their anxiety,
          Prowl car creak & halt:

Today a woman, 20, slapped her brother
                    playing with his infant bricks—
                    toying with a huge rock—
                    'Don't do that now! the cops! the cops!'

And there was no cop there—
        I looked around my shoulder—
a pile of crap in the opposite direction.

           Tear gas! Dynamite! Mustaches!
I'll grow a beard and carry lovely
        bombs,
I will destroy the world, slip in between
           the cracks of death
      And change the Universe—Ha!
I have the secret, I carry
          Subversive salami in
                my ragged briefcase
'Garlic, Poverty, a will to Heaven,'
    a strange dream in my meat:

Radiant clouds, I have heard God's voice in
        my sleep, or Blake's awake, or my own or
the dream of a delicatessen of snorting cows
        and bellowing pigs—
           The chop of a knife
        a finger severed in my brain—

          O brothers of the Laurel
Is the world real?
          Is the Laurel
a joke or a crown of thorns?—

        Fast, pass
        up the ass
        Down I go
        Cometh Woe

—the street outside,
         me spying on New York.
The dark truck passes snarling &
         vibrating deep—

What
    if
        the
            worlds
            were
            a
              series
                    of steps

                        What
                    if
                    the
                    steps
              joined
        back
      at
    the
Margin

Leaving us flying like birds into Time
         —eyes and car headlights—
        The shrinkage of emptiness
in the Nebulae

These Galaxies cross like pinwheels & they pass
          like gas—
What forests are born.

September 15, 1959

TO AN OLD POET IN PERU

Because we met at dusk
Under the shadow of the railroad station
                    clock
While my shade was visiting Lima
And your ghost was dying in Lima
            old face needing a shave
And my young beard sprouted
            magnificent as the dead hair
                    in the sands of Chancay
Because I mistakenly thought you were
                    melancholy
Saluting your 60 year old feet
            which smell of the death
                    of spiders on the pavement
And you saluted my eyes
            with your anisetto voice
Mistakenly thinking I was genial
                    for a youth
(my rock and roll is the motion of an
            angel flying in a modern city)
(your obscure shuffle is the motion
                    of a seraphim that has lost
                            its wings)
I kiss you on your fat cheek (once more tomorrow
Under the stupendous Disaguarderos clock)
Before I go to my death in an airplane crash
            in North America (long ago)
And you go to your heart-attack on an indifferent
                    street in South America
(Both surrounded by screaming

                communists with flowers
                        in their ass)
—you much sooner than I—
                or a long night alone in a room
                in the old hotel of the world
                        watching a black door
                . . . surrounded by scraps of paper

        DIE GREATLY IN THY SOLITUDE
Old Man,
        I prophesy Reward

Vaster than the sands of Pachacamac
Brighter than a mask of hammered gold
Sweeter than the joy of armies naked
                fucking on the battlefield
Swifter than a time passed between
            old Nasca night and new Lima
                    in the dusk
Stranger than our meeting by the Presidential
            Palace in an old cafe
ghosts of an old illusion, ghosts
            of indifferent love—

        THE DAZZLING INTELLIGENCE

            Migrates from Death
To make a sign of Life again to you
Fierce and beautiful as a car crash
        in the Plaza de Armas

I swear that I have seen that Light
I will not fail to kiss your hideous cheek
   when your coffin's closed

And the human mourners go back
    to their old tired
     Dream.

And you wake in the Eye of the
   Dictator of the Universe.

Another stupid miracle! I'm
    mistaken again!
Your indifference! my enthusiasm!
   I insist! You cough!
Lost in the wave of Gold that
   flows thru the Cosmos.

Agh I'm tired of insisting! Goodby,
   I'm going to Pucallpa
to have Visions.
     Your clean sonnets?
I want to read your dirtiest
   secret scribblings,
     your Hope,
in His most Obscene Magnificence. My God!

May 19, 1960

Note: *Chancay, Pachacamic, Nasca—Pre-incaic
   cultures of coastal desert Peru. Myriad relics
   found by graverobbers opening the sand of
   these necropolises.*

AETHER

4 Sniffs & I'm High,
Underwear in bed,
       white cotton in left hand,
   archtype degenerate,
       bloody taste in my mouth
         of Dentist Chair
   music, Loud Farts of Eternity—
an owl with eyeglasses scribbling in the
   cold darkness—
All the time the sound in my eardrums
         of trolleycars below
   taxi fender cough—creak of streets—
   Laughter & pistol shots echoing
         at all walls—
     tic leaks of neon—the voice of Myriad
         rushers of the Brainpan
   all the chirps the crickets have created
   ringing against my eares in the
           instant before unconsciousness
         before,—
     the teardrop in the eye to come,—
     the Fear of the Unknown—

One does not yet know whether Christ was
        God or the Devil—
   Buddha is more reassuring.

Yet the experiments must continue!

Every possible combination of Being—all
the old ones! all the old Hindu
Sabahadabadie-pluralic universes
ringing in Grandiloquent
Bearded Juxtaposition,
with all their minarets and moonlit
towers enlaced with iron
or porcelain embroidery,
all have existed—
and the Sages with
white hair who sat crosslegged on
a female couch—
hearkening to whatever music came
from out the Wood or Street,
whatever bird that whistled in the
Marketplace,
whatever note the clock struck to say
Time—
whatever drug, or aire, they breathed
to make them think so deep
or simply hear what passed,
like a car passing in the 1960 street
beside the Governmental Palace
in Peru, this Lima
year I write.
Kerouac! I salute yr
wordy beard. Sad Prophet!
Salutations and low bows from
baggy pants and turbaned mind and hornèd foot
arched eyebrows & Jewish Smile—
One single specimen of Eternity—each
of us poets.

Breake the Rhythm! (too much pentameter)
　　　　　. . . My god what solitude are you in Kerouac
　　　　　　　　now?
—heard the whoosh of carwheels in the 1950 rain—

And every bell went off on time,
And everything that was created
Rang especially in view of the Creation
For
This is the end of the creation
This is the redemption Spoken of
This is the view of the Created
　　　by all the Drs, nurses, etc of
　　　　　　　　creation;

i.e.,—

!!

> I just nodded because of the secondary
>
> negation

　　　　　　The unspeakable passed over my head for
　　　　　　　　the second time.
　　　　　　　　　　and still can't say it!

　　　i.e. we are the sweepings of the moon
　　　we're what's *left over* from perfection—
　　　The universe is an OLD mistake
　　　I've understood a million times before
　　　and always come back to the same
　　　　　　　　scissor brainwave—
　　　The
　　　Sooner or later all Consciousness will
　　　　　　be eliminated

because Consciousness is
a by-product of—
(Cotton & N_2O)

Drawing saliva back from the tongue—

Christ! you struggle to understand
One consciousness
& be confronted with Myriads—
after a billion years
with the same ringing in the ears
and pterodactyl-smile of Oops
Creation,
known it all before.
A Buddha as of old, with sirens of
whatever machinery making cranging noises in
the street
and pavement light reflected in the facade
RR Station window in a
dinky port in Backwash
of the murky old forgotten
fabulous whatever
Civilization of
Eternity,—
with the RR Sta Clock ring midnight,
as of now,
& waiting for the 6th
you write your
Word,
and end on the last chime—and remember
This *one* twelve was struck
before,
and *never again;* both.

. . . . .I stood on the balcony
              waiting for an explosion
     of Total Consciousness of the All—
              being Ginsberg sniffing ether in Lima.
     The same struggle of Mind, to reach the
                   Thing
     that ends its process with an X
                   comprehending its befores and afters,
     unexplainable to each, except in a prophetic
                   secret recollective hidden
                             half-hand unrecorded.
                                   way.
As the old sages of Asia, or the white beards of Persia
              scribbled on the margins of their scrolls
                   in delicate ink
     remembering with tears the ancient clockbells of their
                                             cities
              and the cities that had been—
              Nasca, Paracas, Chancay & Secrecy of the Priests
                   buried, Cat Gods
              of all colors, a funeral shroud
                   for a museum—
None remember but all return to the same thought
                   before they die—what sad old
              knowledge, we repeat again.
                        Only to be lost
     in the sands of Paracas, or wrapped in a mystic shroud
              of Poesy
     and found by some kid in a thousand years
              inspire what dreadful thoughts of his own?

It's a horrible, lonely experience. And
     Gregory's letter, and Peter's . . .

88

. . . In the foul dregs of Circumstance
     'Male and Female He created them'
       with mustaches.
     There ARE certain REPEATED
     (pistol shot) reliable points
     of reference which the insane
     (pistol shot repeated outside
     the window)—madman suddenly
     writes—THE PISTOL SHOT
     outside—the REPEATED situations
     the experience of return to the
     same place in Universal Creation
     Time—and every time we return
     we recognise again that we
     HAVE been here & that is the
     Key to Creation—the same pistol shot
     —DOWN, bending over his book of Un
     intelligible marvels with his mustache.

(my) Madness is intelligible reactions to
     Unintelligible phenomena.
            Boy—what a marvellous bottle,
      a clear glass sphere of transparent
                        liquid ether—

(Chloraethyl Merz)

9 PM

     I know I am a poet—in this universe—but what
good does that do—when in another, without these mechanical
aids, I might be doomed to be a poor Disneyan Shoe Store
Clerk—This consciousness an *accident* of one of the Ether-

possible worlds, not the Final World

> Wherein we all look Crosseyed
> & triumph in our Virginity
> without wearing Rabbit's-foot
>> ears or eyes looking sideways
>> strangely but in Gold

> Humbled & more knowledgeable, acknowledge
> the Vast mystery of our creation—
> without giving any sign that
>> we have heard from the

GREAT CREATOR

WHOSE NAME I NOW

PRONOUNCE:

GREAT CREATOR OF THE UNIVERS, IF
THY WISDOM ACCORD IT
AND IF THIS NOT BE TOO
MUCH TO ASK
MAY I PUBLISH YOUR NAME?
I ASK IN THE LIMA
NIGHT

FEARFULLY WAITING

ANSWER,

hearing the buses out on
the street hissing,
Knowing the Terror
of the World Afar—

I have been playing with Jokes
and His is too mighty to hold
in the hand like a Pen
and His is the Pistol Shot Answer
that brings blood to the brain
And—

What *can* be possible
in a minor universe
in which you can see
God by sniffing the
gas in a cotton?
The answer to be taken in
reverse & Doubled Math
ematically *both* ways.

Am I a sinner?
There are hard & easy universes. This
is neither.

(If I close my eyes will I regain consciousness?)
That's the Final Question—with
all the old churchbells ringing and
bus pickup snuffles & crack of iron

whips inside cylinders & squeal of brakes
and old crescendos of responsive
demiurgic ecstasy whispering in streets of ear
    —and when was it Not
    ever answered in the Affir-
    mative? Saith the Lord?

A MAGIC UNIVERSE

Flies & crickets & the sound of buses & my
    stupid beard.
But what's Magic?
Is there Sorrow in Magic?
Is Magic one of my boyscout creations?
Am I responsible? I with my flop?
Could Threat happen to Magic?
Yes! this the one universe in which
    there *is* threat to magic. by
    writing while high.

A Universe in which I am condemned to write statements.

'Ignorant Judgements Create Mistaken Worlds—'
    and this one is joined in
        Indic union to
    Affirm with laughing
                eyes—
The world is as we see it,
    Male & Female, passing thru the years,
    as has before & will, perhaps
with all its countless pearls & Bloody noses
    and I poor stupid All in G
    am stuck with that old Choice—

Ya, Crap, what Hymn to seek, & in
　　　　what tongue, if this's the most
　　　　I can requite from Consciousness?—
That I can skim? & put in words?
　　　　　　Could skim it faster with more juice—
　　could skim a crop with Death, perchance
　　　　　　　　—yet never know in this old world.
Will know in Death?
　　　　　　　And before?

　　　　　　　　　　　　　　Will in
Another know.
　　　　　　　And in another know.
　　　　　　　　　　　　　　And
in another know.
　　　　　　　And

　　　　　　　　　　Stop conceiving worlds!
　　　　　　　says Philip Whalen
(My Savior!)　　　　　　　(oh what snobbery!)
　　　　(as if he cd save Anyone)—
　　At *least,* he won't understand.
I lift my finger in the air to create
a universe he won't understand, full
　　　　　of sadness.

—finally staring straight ahead in surprise
　　& recollection into the mirror of
　　　　　the Hotel Commercio room.
　　　　　Time repeats itself. Including
this consciousness, which has seen
itself before—thus the locust-whistle
of antiquity's nightwatch in my eardrum . . .

I propounded a final question, and
    heard a series of final answers.
What is God? for instance, asks the answer?
    And whatever else can the replier reply but reply?
Whatever the nature of mind, that
        the nature of *both* question and answer.

           & yet one wants to live
       in a *single* universe

                    Does one?

Must it be one?
    Why, as with the Jews
  must the God be One?
      O what does
  the concept ONE mean?
      IT'S MAD!

    GOD IS ONE!

      IS X

    IS MEANINGLESS—

      ADONOI—

  IS A JOKE—

    THE HEBREWS ARE

WRONG—(CRIST & BUDDA

ATTEST, also wrongly!)

What is One but Formation
of mind?
arbitrary madness! 6000 years
Spreading out in all directions simultaneously—

I forgive both good & ill
& I seek nothing, like a painted savage with
spear crossed by orange black & white bands!
'I found the Jivaros & was
entrapped in their universe'
I'm scribbling nothings.
Page upon page of profoundest nothing,
as scribed the Ancient Hebe, when
he wrote Adonoi Echad or One—
all to amuse, make money, or deceive—
Let Wickedness be Me
and this the worst of all
the universes!
Not the worst! Not Flame!
I can't stand that — (Yes that's
for Somebody Else!
Yet I accept
O Catfaced God, whatever comes! It's me!
I am the Flame, etc.
O Gawd!
Pistol shot! Crack!
Circusmaster's whip—
IMPERFECT!
and a soul is damned to
HELL!
And the churchbell rings!
and there is melancholy, once again, throughout the realm.

and I'm that soul, small as it is.

HAVE FELT SAME BEFORE

The death of consciousness is terrible
               and yet! when all is ended
                        what regret?
'S none left to remember or forget.
                    And's gone into the odd.
             The only thing I fear is the Last
Chance. I'll see that last chance too
before I'm done, Old Mind. All them
old Last Chances that you knew before.
                    —someday thru the dream wall
        to nextdoor consciousness
               like thru this blue hotel wall
                    —millions of hotel rooms fogging
                        the focus of my eyes—

with whatever attitude I hold the cotton
to my nose, it's still a secret joke
        with pinky akimbo, or with effete queer
             eye in mirror at myself,
             or serious-brow mein
                        & darkened beard,
    I'm still the kid of obscene chance await-
                    ing—
               breathing in a chinese Universe
             thru the nose like some old Brahmanic God.

             O   BELL   TIME   RING   THY
             MIDNIGHT FOR THE BILLIONTH
             SOUNDY TIME, I HEAR AGAIN!

SOUNDY TIME, I HEAR AGAIN!

I'll go walk the street,

Who'll find
me in the night, in Lima, in my
33'd year,

On Street (Cont.)

The souls of Peter &
I answer each other.
But—and what's a soul?
To be a poet's a
serious occupation,
condemned to that
in universe—
to walk the city
ascribbling in
a book—just accosted
by a drunk—
in Plaza de Armas
sidestreet under
a foggy sky, and
sometimes with no
moon.
    The heavy balcony
hangs over the white
marble of the Bishop's
Palace next the Cathedral—
The fountain plays
in light as e'er—
The busses & the

motorcyclists pass
thru midnight, the
carlights shine
the beggar turns
a corner with his
cigarette stub &
cane, the Noisers
leave the tavern
and delay, conversing
in high voice,
Awake,
    Hasta Mañana
they all say—
    and somewhere
at the other end of
the line, a telephone
is ringing, once again
with unknown news—
    The night
looms over Lima,
sky black fog—
and I sit helpless
smoking with a
pencil hand—
    The long crack

in the pavement
        or yesterday's
volcano in Chile,
or the day before
the Earthquake
that begat the
World.

    The Plaza pavement
shines in the electric
light. I wait.
        The lonely beard
workman staggers
home to bed from
Death.
        Yes but I'm
a little tired of
being alone . . .
    Keats' Nightingale—the
instant of realization
a single consciousness
that hears the chimes
of Time, repeated
endlessly—

All night, w / Ether, wave

after wave of magic
understanding. A dis-
turbance of the field
of consciousness.
Magic night, magic stars,
magic men, magic music,
magic tomorrow, magic death,
magic Magic.
        What crude Magic
we live in (seeing trolley
like a rude monster
in downtown street
w / electric diamond
wire antennae to sky
pass night café under
white arc-light by
Gran Hotel Bolivar.)

The mad potter of
Mochica made a
pot w / 6 Eyes & 2
Mouths & half a Nose
& 5 Cheeks & no Chin
for us to figure out,
serious side-track,
blind alley Kosmos.

(Back in Room)

How strange to remember anything, even a button
                much less a universe.
'What creature gives birth to itself?'

The universe is mad, slightly mad.
   —and the two sides wriggle away
   in opposite directions to die
       lopped off
  the blind metallic length curled up
  feebly & wiggling its feet
       in the grass
  the millepede's black head moving inches away
    on the staircase at Macchu Picchu
    the Creature feels itself
       destroyed,
   head & tail of the universe
    cut in two.

Men with slick mustaches of mystery have
   pimp horrible climaxes & Karmas—
—the mad magician that created Chaos
   in the peaceful void & suave.
  with my fucking suave manners & knowitall
    eyes, and mind full of fantasy—
  the Me! that horror that keeps me conscious
   in this Hell of Birth & Death.

   34 coming up—I suddenly felt old—sitting with Walter & Raquel in Chinese Restaurant—they kissed—I alone —age of Burroughs when we first met.

Hotel Commercio
Lima, Peru
May 28, 1960

CITY LIGHTS PUBLICATIONS

Ferlinghetti, Lawrence. LEAVES OF LIFE

Ferlinghetti, Lawrence. PICTURES OF THE GONE WORLD

Ferlinghetti, Lawrence. SEVEN DAYS IN NICARAGUA LIBRE

Finley, Karen. SHOCK TREATMENT

Ford, Charles Henri. OUT OF THE LABYRINTH: Selected Poems

Franzen, Cola, transl. POEMS OF ARAB ANDALUSIA

García Lorca, Federico. ODE TO WALT WHITMAN & OTHER POEMS

García Lorca, Federico. POEM OF THE DEEP SONG

Gascoyne, David. A SHORT SURVEY OF SURREALISM

Ginsberg, Allen. HOWL & OTHER POEMS

Ginsberg, Allen. KADDISH & OTHER POEMS

Ginsberg, Allen. REALITY SANDWICHES

Ginsberg, Allen. PLANET NEWS

Ginsberg, Allen. THE FALL OF AMERICA

Ginsberg, Allen. MIND BREATHS

Ginsberg, Allen. PLUTONIAN ODE

Goethe, J. W. von. TALES FOR TRANSFORMATION

H.D. (Hilda Doolittle). NOTES ON THOUGHT & VISION

Hayton-Keeva, Sally, ed. VALIANT WOMEN IN WAR AND EXILE

Herron, Don. THE LITERARY WORLD OF SAN FRANCISCO

Higman, Perry, transl. LOVE POEMS FROM SPAIN AND
    SPANISH AMERICA

Jaffe, Harold. EROS: Anti-Eros

Kerouac, Jack. BOOK OF DREAMS

Kerouac, Jack. SCATTERED POEMS

Lacarrière, Jacques. THE GNOSTICS

La Duke, Betty. COMPANERAS: Women, Art & Social Change in
    Latin America

La Loca, ADVENTURES ON THE ISLE OF ADOLESCENCE

Lamantia, Philip. MEADOWLARK WEST

Lamantia, Philip. BECOMING VISIBLE

Laughlin, James. THE MASTER OF THOSE WHO KNOW

Laughlin, James. SELECTED POEMS: 1935-1985

Le Brun, Annie. SADE: On the Brink of the Abyss

Lowry, Malcolm. SELECTED POEMS

Marcelin, Philippe-Thoby. THE BEAST OF THE HAITIAN HILLS

Masereel, Frans. PASSIONATE JOURNEY

Moore, Daniel. BURNT HEART

Mrabet, Mohammed. THE BOY WHO SET THE FIRE
Mrabet, Mohammed. THE LEMON
Mrabet, Mohammed. LOVE WITH A FEW HAIRS
Mrabet, Mohammed. M'HASHISH
Murguia, A. & B. Paschke, eds. VOLCAN: Poems from Central America
Paschke, B. & D. Volpendesta, eds. CLAMOR OF INNOCENCE
Pessoa, Fernando. ALWAYS ASTONISHED
Pasolini, Pier Paolo. ROMAN POEMS

Poe, Edgar Allan. THE UNKNOWN POE
Porta, Antonio. KISSES FROM ANOTHER DREAM
Purdy, James. IN A SHALLOW GRAVE
Purdy, James. GARMENTS THE LIVING WEAR
Prévert, Jacques. PAROLES: Selected Poems
Rey-Rosa, Rodrigo. THE BEGGAR'S KNIFE
Rigaud, Milo. SECRETS OF VOODOO
Rips, Geoffrey, ed. UNAMERICAN ACTIVITIES
Saadawi El, Nawal. MEMOIRS OF A WOMAN DOCTOR
Sawyer-Lauçanno, Christopher, transl. THE DESTRUCTION OF
    THE JAGUAR
Sclauzero, Mariarosa. MARLENE
Serge, Victor. RESISTANCE
Shepard, Sam. MOTEL CHRONICLES
Shepard, Sam. FOOL FOR LOVE & THE SAD LAMENT OF
    PECOS BILL
Smith, Michael. IT A COME
Snyder, Gary. THE OLD WAYS
Solnit, Rebecca. SECRET EXHIBITION: Six California Artists
Solomon, Carl. MISHAPS PERHAPS
Tutuola, Amos. FEATHER WOMAN OF THE JUNGLE
Tutuola, Amos. SIMBI & THE SATYR OF THE DARK JUNGLE
Valaoritis, Nanos. MY AFTERLIFE GUARANTEED
Wilson, Colin. POETRY AND MYSTICISM